THE POWER OF CARING

An Everyday Devotional for Pastors, Ministry Leaders, Layleaders, Doctors, Nurses, Nurse Assistants, Healthcare Workers, and Christians who desire to Care for God's People

DR. PETER Z.M. NEHSAHN

outskirts press

This Devotional is dedicated to all Christians Caring for others.

———— ♦ ————

"Life's most persistent and urgent question is, 'What are you doing for others?'"

Dr. Martin Luther King, Jr.

Table of Contents

Introduction

Caring is the hallmark of the Christian faith. It is the source of our joy, and the fulfillment of Christ's law (Gal 6.2). It is also the out-pouring of His love in our hearts. Through caring God provides for the needs of Christians and others who cannot do so themselves. The Apostle Paul writes, "Carry each other's burdens and in this way you will fulfill the law of Christ" (Gal 6.2; NIV).

My call to the ministry and the ongoing commitment to serve God was motivated by caring for others. Therefore, to call myself a Christian, and then neglect to care for the needs of others will be nothing, but mediocrity. Caring is a sacrifice and service. Christ came to render service and give Himself as a sacrificial Lamb for all. His sacrifice and service were motivated by care, love and compassion.

In the pages of this book, you will see that there is power in caring for others. This power of caring is available to you and myself when we accept Jesus Christ who first cared for us.

God Himself demonstrated His caring love for us by sending His one and only Son to die on our behalf (Rom 5.8). God's caring love was clearly demonstrated at the Cross on Calvary. Start caring today and you will be amazed at the difference you will make in the lives of others.

Growing Through Caring

"Brethren, I do not count myself to have apprehended; but one thing I do, forgetting those things which are behind and reaching forward to those things which are ahead, I press toward the goal for the prize of the upward call of God in Christ Jesus" (Philippians 3.13-14).

"Now David said, "Is there still anyone who is left of the house of Saul that I may show him kindness for Jonathan's sake?" And there was a servant of the house of Saul whose name was Ziba. So when they had called him to David, the king said to him, "Are you Ziba?" He said, "At your service!" Then the king said, "Is there not still someone of the house of Saul to whom I may show the kindness of God?" And Ziba said to the king, "There is still a son of Jonathan who is lame in his feet." So the king said to him, "Where is he?" And Ziba said to the king, "Indeed he is in the house of Machir the son of Ammiel, in Lo Debar." Then King David sent and brought him out of the house of Machir the son of Ammiel, from Lo Debar. Now when Mephibosheth the son of Jonathan, the son of Saul had come to David, he fell on his face and prostrated himself. Then David said, "Mephibosheth?" And he answered, "Here is your servant!" So David said to him, "Do not fear, for I will surely show you kindness for Jonathan your father's sake, and will restore to you all the land of Saul your grandfather; and you shall eat bread at my table continually." Then he bowed himself and said, "What is your servant that you should look upon such a dead dog as I" (2 Samuel 9.1-8)?

"The exhorter, in exhortation; the giver, in generosity; the leader, in diligence; the compassionate, in cheerfulness" (Romans 12.8; NRSV).

There Is Excitement in Caring for Others

A minster told a story of going to the war ravaged West African country of Liberia several years ago and picking up a kid off the street and adopting him. The boy's mother had died at birth and his father killed during the civil war. The boy wanted to go to school, but there is no one to help or care for him.

Naming a child in West Africa is a ceremonial affair. Since the boy's parents were not alive to give him a name, he called himself Blamo Doe. This is how he picked his name. One day he was listening to school kids reading a text book. One of the characters in the book was called Blamo Doe. As soon as he heard it, he said, "From now on, my name is Blamo Doe!"

The minister concluded, "Caring means sharing, and sharing brings out the joy and excitement of caring. The more you care and share, the more you grow and become great."

Many people may falsely assume that by not caring or giving

to others, they can secure or hoard their resources for themselves. Our Lord said, "Give, and it shall be given to you: good measure, pressed down, shaken together, and running over" (Luke 6.38). To refuse or avoid caring is disobeying God. Start caring today and you be abundantly blessed by God. And ask God today to help you care for others by sharing. You will grow spiritually, materially, emotionally and otherwise.

Lord, help me focus on caring for others. Help me grow as I care and share with others. Amen!

--------◆--------

"Behold, I do not lecture or a little charity, when I give I give myself."

--Walt Whitman

"One man gives freely, yet gains even more; another withholds unduly, but comes to poverty. A generous man will prosper; he who refreshes others will himself be refreshed" (Proverbs 11.24-25; NIV).

"Now all who believed were together and had all things in common, and sold their possessions and goods and divided them among all as anyone had need. So continuing daily with one accord in the temple and breaking bread from house to house, they ate their food with gladness and simplicity of heart, praising God and having favor with all the people. And the Lord added to the church daily those who were being saved" (Acts 2.44-47).

The Deeper You Care, the Greater You Become

As a kid I fractured my big toe while playing soccer. This was just the beginning of many foot injuries to come. There were no doctors around, so the herbalist came before the cock crowed to pull on the fractured parts. This herbalist was my uncle and his grip was more powerful than any kid could imagine. When he gripped my fractured big toe, my mother reached out to me, and said, "wrap yourself around my waist, and it will not hurt so bad." Her presence reassured me that in spite of the pain, my mother was always there. Her presence soothed my heart that she cared deeply about me. To me that is one of the greatest pictures of God who cares deeply. Through His Spirit, He says, "Cast all your care on me because I care" (I Pet 5.7; paraphrase mine).

In the early church, Christians cared so deeply for each other that they were willing to sell their possessions in order to share with those in need. When they did, God added to their numbers, and the Gospel spread throughout the known world.

If you desire your church to make an impact and become, even greater, try showing compassion to those around you. You will be amazed at what God can do through caring. *Personally, I believe if you desire to care, you definitely have something special to give.*

Lord, give me the desire to care. I know by caring I can become great in You. You first cared for me. Amen!

---◆---

"*Great lives never go out. They go on.*"

−Benjamin Harrison

"Blessed be the God and Father of our Lord Jesus Christ, the Father of mercies and God of all comfort, who comforts us in all our tribulation that we may be able to comfort those who are in any trouble, with the comfort with which we ourselves are comforted by God" (2 Corinthians 1.3-4).

"Now concerning the ministering to the saints, it is superfluous for me to write to you; for I know your willingness about which I boast of you to the Macedonians that Achaia was ready a year ago; and your zeal has stirred up the majority. Yet I have sent the brethren lest our boasting of you should be in vain in this respect that, as I said, you may be ready; lest if *some* Macedonians come with me and find you unprepared, we (not to mention you!) Should be ashamed of this confident boasting. Therefore, I thought it necessary to exhort the brethren to go to you ahead of time and prepare your generous gift beforehand, which you had previously promised that it may be ready as a matter of generosity and not as a grudging obligation" (2 Corinthians 9.1-5).

Your Response to the Needs of Others

Have you been so hung up on trying to figure out why and how to care until you have missed an opportunity to respond to the needs of others? Has the busyness of this life caused you not to live up to your promises of caring for others? None of us can avoid the busyness of this life. Sometimes it seems as though there are only eight rather than twenty-four hours in a day. But it is rewarding to respond adequately, promptly or timely to the needs of others.

When you respond correctly to the immediate and long terms needs of your church, other Christian groups, and even those outside the church, you will begin to understand why it is so important to care. Others will always boast of your generosity and express confidence in your ability to respond to the needs of others. And your caring light will shine so your Father in heaven will be glorified (Matt 5.16).

Forgive me, Lord, for not responding adequately, promptly

or timely to the needs of others. Help me express my confidence in you through generous caring. Amen!

———————•◆•———————

"The only things we ever keep are what we give away."

-—Louis Ginsberg

"Share in suffering like a good soldier of Christ Jesus. No one serving in the army gets entangled in everyday affairs; the soldier's aim is to please the enlisting officer" (2 Timothy 2.3-4; NRSV).

"We know that we have come to know Him if we obey His commands" (1 John 2.3; NIV).

God Is Searching for a Few Good Caring Christians

When I entered nursing school in the late seventies, I took nursing care personally beyond the call of my duty. Caring for the physical, emotional, spiritual, and psychological needs is twenty-four-seven, 365 days' challenge. I gladly accepted the challenge. When I did, God helped me to minister to patients through songs, sharing Christ, reading Scriptures, and rendering physical care. Caring in itself has a therapeutic effect. I even served as an assistant to the hospital chaplain. Through it all, God helped me to matured and grow not only as a nurse, but also as a caring Christian.

The director of the nursing school was so pleased that she and her staff created the Florence Nightingale Award. I was the first recipient. The director was proud because one of her enlisted soldiers lived up to his calling. He did not entangle himself with the affairs of the healthy, and neglect the care of the sick.

To care, a caring Christian must put aside any hindrance in order to care effectively. There are two types of people in this world: those who care, and those who don't care. They may not admit it verbally, but their actions speak louder than their words. The former group rejoice in caring, knowing that He who is in them is greater than the one who is in the latter group (I John 4.4).

Today, God is searching for a few good caring Christians. Will you respond to the call of the Commander-in-Chief of the Lord's army of caregivers? If your respond is "Yes," you may not only know Christ more, but others will respond by accepting Him when they see Him through caring.

Lord, help me to respond to Your call to serve in your army of caregivers. So that I may please You, give me wisdom to avoid getting entangled in the affairs of this life. Amen!

———— • ————

"*If a man cannot be a Christian in the place where he is, he cannot be a Christian anywhere.*"

—Henry Ward Beecher

"And as Christ's soldier do not let yourself become tied up in worldly affairs, for then you cannot satisfy the one who has enlisted you in His army" (2 Timothy 2.4; TLB).

"Then Jesus went about all the cities and villages, teaching in their synagogues, preaching the gospel of the kingdom and healing every sickness and every disease among the people. But when He saw the multitudes, He was moved with compassion for them because they were weary and scattered like sheep having no shepherd" (Matthew 9.35-36).

"Let him who stole, steal no longer, but rather let him labor, working with his hands what is good that he may have something to give him who has need" (Ephesians 4.28).

Allow God to Increase Your Wisdom
in Identifying the Needs of Others

In the late 1990's and early 2000's when Liberian refugees were returning to their civil war ravaged country of Liberia, West Africa, their greatest needs were shelters; even tents in order to keep dried during the raining reason (April-October). Fortunately, other refugees who acquired skills in building construction identified and responded to those needs. Kollie Barco, one of the skilled refugees led a four-man team. As they helped in rebuilding houses for the returnees, Barco and his men were recognized and hired by the United Nations High Commissioner for Refugees (UNHCR).

When a reporter asked Kollie Barco about his desire to help others, and subsequent winning of contract with UNHCR, he replied, "The assistance we rendered our community helped us to land this contract" (*UNHCR, Liberia*; 10 March 2005).

God gives us diverse gifts and talents with the responsibility to invest these resources in His kingdom for His glory. The wise and productive use of our God-given talents yields fruit, joy, and glory for God. (Matt 25.14-30).

At salvation God gives us a new life and identity. He transforms us within. As we mature, He gives us chance to turn our doctrine into practice through fellowship with other Christians. Care is never given apart from fellowship. Through fellowship we are able to identify the needs of others.

Caring also involves interaction with others. The best caring Christians are those who practice their caring skills and are involved in the lives of others.

Lord, give me wisdom to identify and respond to the needs of others. Amen!

———————•◆•———————

Life's most persistent and urgent question is, What are you doing for others?

—Martin Luther King Jr.

Taking Fear Out of the Caring Business

"And do not fear those who kill the body but cannot kill the soul. But rather fear Him who is able to destroy both soul and body in hell" (Matthew 10.28).

"I sought the Lord, and He heard me and delivered me from all my fears" (Ps 34.4).

"For God has not given us a spirit of fear, but of power and of love and of a sound mind" (2 Timothy 1.7).

"There is no fear in love; but perfect love casts out fear because fear involves torment. But he who fears has not been made perfect in love" (1 John 4.18).

Fear May Stop You from Caring for Someone

I know a caring lady who is a nurse assistant. She tells a story about caring for a family friend who turned out to be her worst enemy on the job. This family friend is without a job and goes to her for help. Because the nurse assistant cares, she pleads with her boss to hire the family friend.

When she is hired, she tells the nurse assistant's boss how bad she [nurse assistant] does the job. She [family friend] is the ideal person for the job because the nurse assistant is not qualified. In fact, the nurse assistant does not need any job because she and her husband are rich.

The nurse assistant tells me that she is afraid to care for family members or friends because it usually backfires. My response to her is, Faith in Jesus Christ and commitment to Him should show itself by the actions of care-giving Christians who help in every tangible way. Therefore, you are no exception. Despite the ingratitude of people, do not be fearful of caring for others.

When it comes to caring, the circumstances do not matter. A caregiver's role of caring does not change with circumstances. God does not call a caregiver to care only when conditions are perfect. In caring you will be on top of the hill and at times you will be at the bottom of the hill. But God can do all things through you for His glory (Phil 4.13).

When you love others and genuinely desire to care for them, the Holy Spirit will help to overcome your fear. He will draw people closer to the Lord and ultimately bring glory to God through caring.

Lord, grant me the spirit of love that embodies fearlessness with a sound mind, ready to care. Amen!

———◆——

"The only thing we have to fear is fear itself."

--President Franklin D. Roosevelt

"Whatever I tell you in the dark, speak in the light; and what you hear in the ear, preach on the housetops. And do not fear those who kill the body but cannot kill the soul. But rather fear Him who is able to destroy both soul and body in hell. Are not two sparrows sold for a copper coin? And not one of them falls to the ground apart from your Father's will. But the very hairs of your head are all numbered. Do not fear therefore; you are of more value than many sparrows" (Matthew 10.27-31).

"But a certain Samaritan, as he journeyed, came where he was. And when he saw him, he had compassion. So he went to him and bandaged his wounds, pouring on oil and wine; and he set him on his own animal and brought him to an inn and **_took care of him_**" (Luke 10.33-34; bold and italic mine).

Overcoming the Fear of Caring

Men and women go to nursing schools in order to learn how to care for the sick. What they learn in the secrets of their classrooms are shown to the world in clinics and hospitals through caring. Most men and women who quit nursing schools are those who cannot stand to look at sick people. Rather than being overcome with compassion, they are overwhelmed with fear by mere sights of suffering people. In other words, fear assaults their compassion.

Pain and suffering expose your own vulnerability and weakness. When that happens, you become fearful and begin to doubt your own ability to care for others. The caring profession is not easy. Caregivers may face difficulties, pain, suffering and sorrow.

In caring situations that may seem impossible, it is understandable for caregivers to be afraid. God told the Israelites not to be afraid or fearful in the face of the battle (Deut 17.17-21).

God asks caregivers to remember or recall what He has done in other caring situations in the past and take heart. Our awesome God who reigns goes into every caring battle with us.

Christ reassures us not to be fearful because the very hairs on our heads are numbered by God, the Father.

The Good Samaritan was not fearful of what he set out to do. He saw a man who had been beaten bloody and left half dead. He immediately went down to the man, poured wine and bandages his wounds. He, then set the bloody man on his own animal and took care of him.

Caring may require dealing with people who are in distress, pains, or who may be terminally ill. Unless you the care-er overcome your own fear, you will not be effective.

Lord, I do desire to care for others, but my own fear does not allow me to be an effective caregiver. Help me overcome it. Amen!

———◆———

"There is no panic on our agenda."

--President Lyndon B. Johnson

"A wicked messenger falls into trouble, but a faithful ambassador brings health" (Proverbs 13.17).

"Assuredly, I say to you, inasmuch as you did it to one of the least of these my brethren, you did it to me" (Matthew 25.40b).

"And when Saul had come to Jerusalem, he tried to join the disciples; but they were all afraid of him and did not believe that he was a disciple. But Barnabas took him and brought him to the apostles. And he declared to them how he had seen the Lord on the road and that He had spoken to him and how he preached boldly at Damascus in the name of Jesus" (Acts 9.26-27).

You Are Christ's Ambassador of Caring

An ambassador goes to another nation to fearlessly represent his or her country. He or she may be called upon to defuse crises that may lead to war between their nations. Whatever the ambassador does may become his or her legacy as a diplomat. Caring, kindness, compassion and sensitivity are hallmarks of a knowledgeable diplomat. A caring diplomat is most likely to win the hearts of the people of the host country.

When the Asian Tsunami struck in December 2004, Christ's ambassadors of caregivers responded immediately. Without fear of personal safeties, or diseases, they scattered throughout Asia doing what they do best; caring for the injured, the homeless, the sick and orphans. They even cared for the dying and dead.

At times Christians may be required to care in a war zone where they may face the danger of being hurt or killed. Satan and his forces have grip on this world, causing untold sufferings around the globe. But our Lord said we need not be afraid because He has already defeated our enemies. Christians can remain firm in their faith that God has called them as caring ambassadors to care for others.

Wherever there are earthquakes, typhoons, hurricanes, or other disasters around the world, Christian caregivers have always been there to defuse tensions and prepare the masses for other relief agencies.

Shortly after his conversion, Saul came to Jerusalem, but the disciples were afraid of him. Barnabas, the encourager, cared so deeply about Saul that he [Barnabas] took and personally introduced him [Saul] to the disciples in Jerusalem.

Lord, I want to be remembered as Your ambassador of caregiver. Help me maintain my status as a compassionate diplomat. Amen!

————— ◆ —————

"Whatever makes men good Christians, makes them good citizens."

-—Daniel Webster

"But the King replied to Araunah, "No, I insist on paying you for it. I will not sacrifice to the Lord my God burnt offerings that cost me nothing" (2 Samuel 24.24; NIV).

"And do not be conformed to this world, but be transformed by the renewing of your mind that you may prove what is that good and acceptable and perfect will of God" (Romans 12.2).

"Therefore, if anyone is in Christ, he is a new creation; old things have passed away; behold all things have become new" (2 Cor 5.17).

"And do not forget to do good and to share with others, for with such sacrifices God is pleased" (Hebrews 13.16; NIV).

Putting the Bad Habits Behind in Order to Care

"I do not know how to care for other people." "I am not much of a caring person." "Caring for other people makes me nervous because I do not know what to expect." "When you care too much, people take advantage of you."

If you make any of the excuses above, you are not along. Because caring requires personal sacrifice on the part of the caregiver, it [caring] can be a difficult decision. Caring may require sacrifice of time, money, manpower, or the very life of the caregiver.

I know old habits die hard. But the Bible says you can be transformed by renewing your mind. When that happens, you are no longer the same. God enables you to do things you have never done before. That includes learning to care as you have never cared before.

Your new acquired habits of caring no longer fit the patterns of what this world considers caring. To the world, giving your used-worn clothes and furniture to others is caring. But a person of new creation says, if it does not require sacrifice that is pleasing to my God, then it is not caring.

Lord, help me get rid of my old habits of excuses of not caring. I know that I am transformed because my mind is renewed. Please accept my sacrificial caring for others. I know this is Your will for me. Amen!

————•◆•————

"Nothing so needs reforming as other people's habits."

–Mark Twain

"Carry each other's burdens, and in this way you will fulfill the law of Christ" (Galatians 6.2).

"And let us not grow weary while doing good, for in due season we shall reap if we do not lose heart. Therefore, as we have opportunity, let us do good to all, especially to those who are of the household of faith" (Galatians 6.9-10).

"But even after we had suffered before and were spitefully treated at Philippi, as you know, we were bold in our God to speak to you the gospel of God in much conflict. For our exhortation did not come from error or uncleanness, nor was it deceit" (1 Thessalonians 2.2-3).

Obeying Christ's Call to Care for Others

When Heather Mercer and Dayna Curry were rescued by the Northern Alliance troops November 15, 2001 in Afghanistan, the young women vowed to return to their mission of caring for the Afghans. After the US Military removed the Talibans, the young women saw an opportunity to make more impact by caring for Afghan women and children.

The value of a Christian's compassion can never be over-emphasized. Anyone may criticize what a Christian does, but it takes a true bold Christian to be compassionate. Showing compassion may be hazardous to a Christian's safety. The caring business is risky and dangerous.

In trouble countries around Africa and Middle East such as Cote D'Ivoire, Ethiopia, Guinea, Iraq, Liberia, South Sudan, Somalia, Syria and Yemen, Christians caregivers have been killed in cross fires in factional fighting or executed by Islamic State (IS) fighters. In fact, wherever there are arm conflicts around the world, the stories are always the same.

We fulfill Christ's law when we boldly bear each other's burdens. The power of caring; Christians lovingly and genuinely meeting the needs of others can never be quenched or defeated through the barrel of a gun.

Lord, grant me boldness in my caregiving so that I may respond to the needs of others no matter how difficult or dangerous the situation. Amen!

———————◆———————

"I'll go where you want me to go, dear Lord, O'er mountain or plain or sea; I'll say what you want me to say, dear Lord, I'll be what you want me to be."

—*Mary Brown*

Strengthening Your
Family Relationships Through Caring

"But anyone does not provide for his own, and especially for those of his household, he has denied the faith and is worse than an unbeliever" (I Timothy 5.8).

"Then Joseph said to his brothers and to his father's household, "I will go up and tell Pharaoh and say to him, my brothers and those of my father's house, who were in the land of Canaan have come to me. And the men are shepherds, for their occupation has been to feed livestock; and they have brought their flocks, their herds and all that they have." So it shall be when Pharaoh calls you and says, what is your occupation? That you shall say, "Your servants' occupation has been with livestock from your youth even till now, both we and also our fathers, that you may dwell in the land of Goshen;" for every shepherd is an abomination to the Egyptians" (Genesis 46.31-34).

"Then Pharaoh spoke to Joseph, saying, "Your father and your brothers have come to you. The land of Egypt is before you. Have your father and brothers dwell in the best of the land; let them dwell in the land of Goshen. And if you know any competent men among them, then make them chief herdsmen over my livestock" (Genesis 47.5-6).

God Can Work Through You in Caring for Your Family

Family caring for each other is as old as the Bible itself. Jesus calls every Christian into the caring business, especially members of the same family. He places every family member on the frontline of caring. No matter how caring other Christians may be, some people prefer to discuss their needs with relatives. Relatives are more accessible than others, and are easier to talk to than strangers.

It is unfortunate that some families are characterized by conflict than by caring and compassion. Joseph's brothers hate him. One day he took food to them while tending sheep. The brothers captured Joseph, put him in a pit and later sold him as a slave to strangers.

The brothers went to Egypt to buy food, and they found themselves standing before Joseph. Immediately he [Joseph] recognized them, but the brothers did not. Joseph cared for them and later brought the entire family to Egypt and resettled them in the land of Goshen; the best of the Egyptian land.

Joseph knew he had been treated unfairly by his own brothers. Yet one thing was important to him; caring and saving lives, including the lives of his own (Gen 50.19-20).

Give me a caring heart, dear Lord. Then, help me live it out in practical reality in my everyday family life. Teach me to serve my family. Amen!

———— ◆ ————

"Nothing is so embarrassing as watching someone do something that you said couldn't be done."

—Sam Ewing

"Behold, how good and how pleasant it is for brethren to dwell together in unity. It is like the precious oil upon the head, running down on the beard of Aaron. Running down on the edge of his garments. It is like the dew of Hermon, descending upon the mountains of Zion; for there the Lord commanded the blessing-life forevermore" (Psalm 133.1-3).

"If someone says, I love God and hates his brother, he is a liar; for he who does not love his brother whom he has seen, how can he love God whom he has not seen? And this command-ment we have from Him: that he who loves God must love his brother also" (1 John 4.20-21).

Family Can Be United Through Caring

A West African family comes to America and resettles in a major city in the Southeast. They keep to themselves, and barely associate with relatives and friends in their community. One day a teenage daughter of the family is tragically killed by a former boyfriend.

The community rises up and responds in an awesome way. The community literally draws the family from their secluded hideouts and cares for them. Other relatives and friends who have been cut off for a long period of time are reunited with the family in sharing their grief and burdens.

There is something magnetically contagious about caring. Caring can reconcile old foes and heal wounds of bitterness. As a pastor I have seen this firsthand.

There is great joy when separated family members reconcile and reunite. It may require forgiveness on the part of some family members to forgive each other for true healing and unity to take place through caring. Notice that one person can forgive, but it takes two people to reconcile. Forgiveness may not necessarily guarantee reconciliation, but it is always a step in the right direction. It soothes the rough edges of the hurts and wrongs done by others (2 Sam 14.33).

If you are not sure how you can unite or reunite your family, try caring for them. Look for an opportunity to carry out random acts of kindnesses, or random acts of senseless kindnesses.

And if you do not know where to begin, pray for your family. Send an encouraging card to a family member who is not expecting one. Drop by with a special gift when a family member least expects it. There is something refreshing about the element of surprise when family care for each other.

Lord, grant me the courage to reach out and unite my family through caring. Amen!

———— ◆ ————

"A house divided against itself cannot stand."

—*Abraham Lincoln*

"Everyone of you shall revere his mother and his father and keep my Sabbath: I am the Lord" (Leviticus 19.3).

"Honor widows who are really widows. But if any widow has children or grandchildren, let them first learn to show piety at home and to repay their parents; for this is good and acceptable before God" (I Timothy 5.3-4).

"But if anyone does not provide for his own, and especially for those of his household, he has denied the faith and is worse than an unbeliever" (I Timothy 5.8).

Your Greatest Treasure Is Caring

Around Mother's Day every year, newspapers across the United States carry articles about men and women who make a difference in the lives of their mothers in caring for them.

An USA Today's article about a thirty-six years old man who came home to care for his seventy-five years old ailing amputee mother touched me. The newspaper quoted the man as saying, "I do not sit on any pedestal, not a day goes by that I am not exhausted and I do not wonder, "when will this ever end"? "But then I remember that so many of my associates have lost their mothers. And I know God put me here for a reason."

What were you doing, or where were you when God called you to care? Simon and Andrew were fishing when Jesus called them to follow Him. The Bible says, "They immediately left their nets and followed Him" (Mark 1.18). Whatever your profession, if God has called you to care, you will have to make a dramatic change. This may require a change of job, priority, location and change of focus. Nothing should ever stop a Christian from responding immediately when the Lord calls.

God put all of us here to care for family members who cannot care for themselves. Caring may require us to move closer to home, change jobs, or change careers.

Every Mother's Day, when you pick up newspapers and read about men and women who are caring for family members, especially mothers, pray and ask God to give the caregivers strength to endure until the end.

And may I add that God surely loves a cheerful caregiver. Caring for family members may not be the easier thing, but it is the right thing to do.

Dear Lord, give me strength and endurance to care for my family. Help me obey Your voice by caring for those of my household. Amen!

————•————

"I'd rather be a failure at something I enjoy than be a success at something I hate."

--—George Burns

"Joseph said to them, "Do not be afraid, for am I in the place of God? But as for you, you meant evil against me; but God meant it for good in order to bring it about as it is this day, to save many people alive. Now therefore, do not be afraid; I will provide for you and your little ones." And he comforted them and spoke kindly to them" (Genesis 50.19-21).

"If there is among you a poor man of your brethren, within any of the gates in your land which the Lord your God is giving you, you shall not harden your heart nor shut your hand from your poor brother, but you shall open your hand wide to him and willingly lend him sufficient for his need, whatever he needs. Beware there be a wicked thought in your heart, saying, "The seventh year, the year of release is at hand; and your eye be evil against your poor brother and you give him nothing, and he cry out to the Lord against you, and it become sin among you. You shall surely give to him, and your heart should not be grieved when you give to him, because for this thing the Lord your God will bless you in all your works and in all to which you put your hand" (Deuteronomy 15.7-10).

Doing the Best for Your Family

A lady tells a story of a West African family that migrated and resettled in the United States about several years ago. The boys are doing quite well. They do have well-paying jobs, and have purchased homes for themselves.

The parents are doing very well also. God has blessed them so much that they have purchased three automobiles and shipped them to their country of origin. They, too have a nice home.

There is a young lady in the family. She is very talented, and desires to pursue a career in singing. The family flatly refuses to help her financially. The parents believe it is the responsibility of their local congregation to underwrite every expense relating to the young lady's singing career. The parents are upset at the local congregation and are threatening to withdraw their fellowship.

If you were a member of this family, what would you do? This is what I would do. I will not only care about my sister's singing career, but I will also help her financially. I will pray for God to open door to her.

God blesses us so that we may be blessings to our own family. If we do, God will continue to prosper whatever we put our hands on.

Lord, I know there is nothing pleasing to You than doing the best for my family. Help me respond to their needs. Amen!

————— ◆ —————

"Well done is better than well said."

—Benjamin Franklin

"He riseth from supper and laid aside His garments; and took a towel and girded Himself. After that He poureth water into a bason and began to wash the disciples' feet and wipe them with the towel wherewith He was girded. So after He had washed their feet and had taken His garments and was set down again, He said unto them, know ye what I have done to you? Ye call me Master and Lord: and ye say well; for so I am. If I then, your Lord and Master have washed your feet; ye also ought to wash one another's feet. For I have given you an example that ye should do as I have done to you" (John 13.4-5, 12-15).

"Owe no one anything except to love one another, for he who loves another has fulfilled the law. Love does no harm to a neighbor; therefore love is the fulfillment of the law" (Romans 13.8, 10).

Fulfilling Your God-Given Role of Caring

My first "Foot Washing Service" was quite an experience. I had intended it to be a live illustration for my message on love and care. I spoke to one of the deacons Saturday night for this illustration. By the way, if you want to wash a church member's feet, choose a deacon. There is nothing as humbling as washing a contemporary deacon's feet.

Before I got through washing his feet, there were at least three others who wanted their feet to be washed. God used the feet washing as a powerful demonstration of love and compassion that I have for His people. Since we call ourselves Caring Believers Bible Fellowship, I wanted to demonstrate to the congregation what we ought to do for each other. Each of us would fulfill his or her role as a caregiver by following Christ's example.

It pleases Christ when family members who call Him Lord and Master fulfill their roles by following His example of caring for each other. There is no greater love than when family care for each other. Family that cares for each other often finds strength, support and healing in every crisis. Caring is incomparably therapeutic, even when a family is facing crisis.

Lord Jesus, thank You for the example You set for us by washing Your disciples' feet. Give me the humility to follow Your example. Amen!

————◆————

"Joy comes from seeing the complete fulfillment of the specific purpose for which I was created and born again, not from successfully doing something of my own choosing."

—Oswald Chambers

"We then who are strong ought to bear with the scruples of the weak and not to please ourselves. Let each of us please his neighbor for his good, leading to edification" (Romans 15.1-2).

"Moreover it is required in stewards that one be found faithful" (1 Corinthians 4.2).

"And above all things have fervent love for one another, for love will cover multitude of sins. As each one has received a gift, minister it to one another as good stewards of the manifold grace of God. If anyone speaks, let him speak as the oracles of God. If anyone ministers, let him do it as with the ability which God supplies, that in all things God may be glorified through Jesus Christ to whom belong the glory and the dominion forever and ever." Amen! (1 Pet 4.8-11).

God Has Chosen You as a Steward

A steward is a person who manages someone else's estate or property. Managing involves taking care of the property in such a way that it reproduces or produces fruit. A manager's skill is evaluated by how much returns the property yields.

In the context of the Christian faith, the gospel has been entrusted to us. The "Great Commission" (Matt 28.19-20), empowers us to make disciples, baptize and teach them to observe all that Christ has entrusted to us. Teaching and discipling cannot be carried apart from caring. A caring Christian's involvement in the lives of others may be a crucial factor in the discipling and maturing process. Being a caring Christian starts with knowing God, His will and showing loving actions toward others. God expects Christians to care and bear each other's burdens (Gal 6.2).

Our Lord and Savior Jesus Christ was the greatest of all teachers because He did not only teach with authority, but taught with compassion, love and care. If you desire to win your family to Christ, present Him as a compassionate and caring Savior who sacrificed His life for them.

Families that care for each other, stay together. When families reach out personally and visibly to each other, they become attractive models for their community in caring and sharing. Family relationships may be built on words, but they [relationships] are cemented with caring. Families, especially Christian families have the awesome responsibility to reflect our Lord in everything they do, including how they care for each other.

Lord, help me be a faithful steward in all that I do. Amen!

————◆————

"When you follow Christ it must be a total burning of all your bridges behind you."

—Billy Graham

"Now Jabez was more honorable than his brothers, and his mother called his name Jabez, saying, "Because I bore him in pain." And Jabez called on the God of Israel saying, "Oh, that you would bless me indeed and enlarge my territory, that your hand would be with me, and that I may not cause pain." So God granted him what he requested" (1 Chronicles 4.9-10).

"And whatever you do in word or deed, do all in the name of the Lord Jesus, giving thanks to God the Father through Him" (Colossians 3.17).

Caring Beyond the Family That Binds

Brother Titus came to the United States in the late 1980's. He and I knew each other quite well. We attended the same church together. In fact, we went to the same Sunday school class and served on the outreach team. While coming from work one day, he was hit by a speeding motorist. He was pronounced brain dead eight hours later at the hospital.

But in death, Titus cared, shared and saved more lives than when he was alive. With his sister's permission, Titus' organs were removed and transplanted in recipients who were waiting for organ donors. A little known West African young man gave second chances at life to other family members who could not even locate his home country of Liberia, West Africa on a map.

It is not enough to be called a caregiver. You must actually make a difference in the lives of others. That is one of the greatest challenges a caregiver may face. It is one thing to be called a caregiver and, it is another thing to actually care or live up to one's name.

Caring has no demarcation. It has no ethnicity, boundaries, or national origin. People who care just do it, even in death.

Like any international who migrates to the great United States, Brother Titus prayed that God would bless him indeed, and enlarge his territory, and that he would cause no pain to someone. But sadly, someone brought pain and death to him. And in his painful death, God used him to save many lives and enlarged his territory.

Lord, in caring for my own family, I want to reach out and touch someone. Help me do it as if unto you. Amen!

———— ◆ ————

"Our heavenly Father never takes anything from His children unless He means to give them something better."

—George Muller

Winning the War of Selfness Within

"Therefore, if anyone is in Christ, he is a new creation; old things have passed away; behold, all things have become new" (2 Corinthians 5.17).

"Nobody should seek his own good, but the good of others" (I Corinthians 10.24; NIV).

"Do nothing from selfish ambition or conceit, but in humility regard others as better than yourselves. Let each of you look not to your own interests, but to the interests of others. Let the same mind be in you that was in Christ Jesus" (Philippians 2.3-5; NRSV).

"Serve one another in Love" (Galatians 5.13b; NIV).

How to Get Rid of Selfness

Most of my early years were spent with missionaries on mission stations in rural Northeastern Liberia. I heard amazing stories about their home countries. I was told that the missionaries had everything at their disposal; electricity, clean water, healthcare, meal three times a day, free education, and a whole lot more.

But I could not understand why missionaries would leave such life and come to the snake infested jungles, mosquitoes infested swamps and AIDS infected prisons of Africa? The reason was simple: they care about God's people. In order to be effective in propagating the Gospel, they have to get rid of self. When self is removed, nothing stands in the path of the missionaries. They will dig their own wells, build their own houses, and even learn to speak the indigenous languages.

A sixty-eight years old missionary who has a prison ministry in West African notorious prisons says to the inmates, "For me, following Jesus meant leaving my five children and 11 grandchildren in the United States. It will cost you, too. But it also will cost you not to follow Him. . . ."

The secret to getting rid of self is to focus on Jesus Christ. He will turn your face where His heart is: with His people.

Lord, thank you for calling me to be caregiver to others. Help me get rid of my selfness and respond to the needs of others. Amen!

———◆———

"Self-preservation is the first principle of our nature."

—*Alexander Hamilton*

"Let no one seek his own, but each one the other's well-being" (I Corinthians 10.24).

"We then who are strong ought to bear with the scruples of the weak and not to please ourselves. Let each of us please his neighbor for his good, leading to edification" (Romans 15.1-2).

Caring Is Not Self-Focused

Satan wants to destroy your ability to care for others. Once he gets you to focus on yourself, you become powerless in responding to the needs of others. Your ability to care is constantly under attack. You may lose one or two battles, but no matter what the case may be, Christ makes you strong to care.

The faithfulness of our God is awesome! When you and I submit to God in all that we desire to do, Satan will flee from us (Jas 4.7). We can do all things; **all caring** through Him because our strengths lie within Him.

A planned and ordered life is a closed life. Such a life focuses exclusively on self. When God calls a man or woman, He [God] gives him or her a servant heart. A servant's heart is transparent and open, willing whenever the Master calls. In order words, a servant is called to care for others.

God calls me to serve others and to seek their well-being.

God calls you to do the same for your neighbors. God does not say anything about self-edification in His Word. You and I can edify others through caring services.

Lord, I know you call me to serve others, but the enemy wants me to focus on myself. I know Satan is a liar. I will submit to you in my desire to care, and he will flee from me. Amen!

————◆————

"*The less I spent on myself and the more I gave to others the fuller of happiness and blessing did my soul become.*"

—Hudson Taylor

"Be on your guard against all kinds of greed; a man's life does not consist in the abundance of his possessions" (Luke 12.15; NIV).

"You who have shown me great and severe troubles, shall revive me again. And bring me up again from the depths of the earth" (Psalm 71.20).

"A kind man benefits himself; but a cruel man brings trouble on himself" (Proverbs 11.17).

"Now we exhort you brethren, warn those who are unruly, comfort the fainthearted, uphold the weak, be patient with all. See that no one renders evil for evil to anyone, but always pursue what is good both for yourselves and for all" (1 Thessalonians 5.14-15).

"If anyone among you thinks he is religious and does not bridle his tongue but deceives his own heart, this one's religion is useless. Pure and undefiled religion before God the Father is this: to visit orphans and widows in their trouble, and to keep oneself unspotted from the world" (James 1.26-27).

The Temptations to Always Care about Oneself

I have had many difficult events throughout my life. I was born into a poor West African family. I lost four brothers to childhood diseases. By age fifteen, I had lost my father, and both maternal grandparents. I received my first pair of pants at age nineteen. By age twenty-five, I had lost both paternal aunts. By age forty, I had lost my first son, both maternal aunts, two paternal uncles and three second cousins. At age fifty-nine, I lost my mother. After the birth of our second son, my wife and I were told that we would never have any more children. Seven years ago I lost my savings in a failed business venture.

When you face the challenges of life, the tendency is to care about your own needs. *Sometimes I just want to take care of me.* If someone does not care, why should I care?

My religion will be in vain if I only care about me. Each day I get call from Liberia to help family and friends who are struggling to make ends meet. Sometimes I am tempted to change my telephone numbers. But knowing God motivates me to care. Caring for the needs of others flows out of knowing God, and draws me, even closer to Him.

Whatever caring job you may be in, you can work as though God were your employer. When that happens, you will care with excellence. Any caring duty you undertake, let the excellency that glorifies God be your hallmark.

Lord, help me overcome the temptations to care about me. But I know you call me to be a blessing to others as you have also blessed me. Amen!

———— ♦ ————

"Only a life lived for others is a life worthwhile."

—Albert Einstein

"Whoever shuts his ears to the cry of the poor will also cry himself and not be heard" (Proverbs 21.13).

"Behold, happy is the man whom God corrects; therefore, do not despise the chastening of the Almighty. For He bruises, but He binds up; He wounds, but His hands make whole. He shall deliver you in six troubles, yes, in seven no evil shall touch you" (Job 5.17-19).

"For we do not wrestle against flesh and blood, but against principalities, against powers, against the rulers of the darkness of this age, against spiritual hosts of wickedness in the heavenly places" (Ephesians 6.12).

"For this is the will of God, that by doing good you may put to silence the ignorance of foolish men" (1 Peter 2.15).

Winning the Battle of Selfishness

My life experiences described in the last section are personal battles. I have been to the mountain top, and I have also been at the bottom of the mountain. I can honestly say that I have been at the bottom of the mountain the better part of my life. But one thing has never changed about my life: my desire to genuinely care for God's people.

I have resisted and fought against the inner desire to be as selfish as possible. I have won every time because God has consistently shown me that caring is not a matter of necessity, but of love.

Caring for God's people is an investment with Him. God takes the plight of His suffering people serious. When God speaks of Christians carrying each other's burdens, He means it.

The need to care for God's people is greater than ever before. As HIV/AIDS, Ebola and Hepatitis continue to kill people at alarming rates in developing countries of Africa and around the world, the need to care has become acute. These diseases may become the most fearsome "Weapons of Mass Destruction" the 21st century world may forever remember.

We fight from victory because Christ has won the battle for us. Therefore, we care from winning over selfishness.

Open my eyes, Lord, so that I can see the needs of others. Help me overcome the inner battle of selfishness to care. Amen!

———— ◆ ————

"Kind words can be short and easy to speak, but their echoes are truly endless."

—*Mother Teresa*

Taking Personal Emotions Out of Caring

"If any of you lacks wisdom, let him ask of God, who gives to all liberally and without reproach, and it will be given to him. But let him ask in faith, with no doubting, for he who doubts is like a wave of the sea driven and tossed by the wind. For let not that man suppose that he will receive anything from the Lord; he is a double-minded man, unstable in all his ways" (James 1.5-8).

"The locusts have no king, yet they all advance in ranks" (Proverbs 30.27).

"So we being many, are one body in Christ, and individually members of one another" (Romans 12.5).

"If the foot should say, because I am not a hand, I am not of the body, is it therefore not of the body? And if the ear should say because I am not an eye, I am not of the body, is it therefore not of the body? If the whole body were an eye, where would be the hearing? If the whole body were hearing, where would be the smelling? But now God has set the members, each one of them in the body just He pleased. And if they were all one member, where would the body be? But now indeed there are many members, yet one body. And the eye cannot say to the hand, I have no need of you; nor again the head to the feet, I have no need of you" (1 Corinthians 12.15-21).

Caring Alone Can Be Difficult

Imagine a high school soccer team with men who are skillful dribblers. In their emotional zeal to please the crowd, they are careless with the ball. They dribble until exhausted, then lose the ball to the enemies.

That's how my high school soccer team was until one day the coach decided to teach us a lesson on team work. He asked us to play one-on-one. If you ever played soccer on a team, never attempt to play one-on-one. Make sure you are in good health, or you will have a heart attack.

In my high school days, lengths of soccer fields depended on the location (city), and population of the high school. My high school was located in the city where the county government resided. It has over a thousand students. Therefore, the field was very long and wide.

Barely twenty minutes into the practice, the coach stopped the play. We couldn't breathe! The coach's main point: soccer is a team sport. If you attempt to play it by yourself, you will always lose.

Christians are most effective in caregiving when they work as teams. Like soldiers, Christian caregivers speak passionately of relationships they develop in battlefields of caring. Men and women who struggle together through difficult conditions will most likely form lifelong friendships with each other. Christians create bonds when they care together saving and making a difference in the lives of others. When you find yourself in the caring trenches, do not lose sight of your co-caregiver who may be standing beside you (Jer 3.55-57).

Jesus Christ is our Coach. We are on His team. He demands and requires team work. Caring is not about pleasing the crowd. It is about doing the will of God.

Lord, help me realize that caring is a team effort, and it is not about pleasing the crowd, doing Your will. Amen!

————— • —————

"*He may not score, and yet he helps to win who makes the hit that brings the runner.*"

—*Arthur Guiterman*

"And I will pray the Father, and He will give you another Helper, that He may abide with you forever—the Spirit of truth, whom the world cannot receive because it neither sees Him nor knows Him; but you know Him for He dwells with you and will be in you" (John 14.16-17).

"Nevertheless I tell you the truth. It is to your advantage that I go away; for if I do not go away, the Helper will not come to you; but if I depart, I will send Him to you" (John 16.7).

"I can do all things through Christ who strengthens me" (Philippians 4.13).

There Is a Helper for You

We live in an era of "Self-help," or "Do-it-yourself." From household appliances to automobiles, there are "Self-help," or "Do-it-yourself kits." We have been trained and groomed to do things by and for ourselves. But the doctrine of self-reliance is a recipe for failure in any caregiving ministry.

You would think that the disciples needed no "Helper" having been with Jesus for three years. They would just do it! After all, they were trained by the Master Himself. But in His parting words," Jesus told His disciples, "And I will pray the Father, and He will give you another Helper that He may abide with you forever" (John 14.16). Jesus was speaking about the Holy Spirit.

If Jesus's disciples needed the Holy Spirit for enablement, how much more do we need Him? Caregiving apart from the power of the Holy Spirit is not likely to go far. There are no quick fixes to caring for others. Caring is done over a long period of time depending on the immediate and long term needs of people to whom care is provided.

And the importance of friendship in the caring business should never be overlooked. God, through the Holy Spirit brings those who care for His people together to have relationships with each other. They can rejoice and celebrate their accomplishments together. When caregivers have a strong relationship with God and strong friendship with each other, they can accomplish great things in caring. Friendships among Christian caregivers are precious in the sight of God. When caring, find a good friend and be good friends (Eccl 4.9-12).

When caring is your passion, you cannot do anything, but ask the "Helper" repeatedly to surround you with best friends, give you the desire and enablement to do your best. Your own emotional strength will fail you.

Dear, Lord, I need the Helper. Be my partner, Holy Spirit. Walk, talk, and guide me every step I take, and every word I utter in my daily caregiving. Amen!

————◆————

"I would rather walk with God in the dark than go alone in the light."

—Mary Gardiner Brainard

"Call to me, and I will answer you and show you great and mighty things which you do not know" (Jeremiah 33.3).

"Likewise the Spirit also helps in our weaknesses. For we do not know what we should pray for as we ought, but the Spirit Himself makes intercession for us with groanings which cannot be uttered. Now He who searches the hearts knows what the mind of the Spirit is because He makes intercession for the Saints according to the will of God" (Romans 8.26-27).

When It Comes to Caring, What Does the Caregiver Look For?

When it comes to caring, you just want to do it. But relying exclusively on your emotions may lead to inadequate respond to a specific need. Caring decision made under emotional duress may not be the best decision.

I come from a Western African culture where many people respond based on their emotional instincts. If a brother loses a job, the community will respond by raising funds. This usually generates a few hundred dollars to buy groceries. Rather than raising a few hundred dollars, what this brother needs is to network with the community in finding an employment.

Again, when a brother or sister is critically ill, friends and families may not care for his or her needs. But as soon as he or she dies, friends and families will rally the community to raise a huge sum of money for burial. May I say that caring for the dead is not the best care ever.

Christians are usually at their best when the Holy Spirit leads them in mapping out caring plans so that they know what to look for, and how to respond.

Solomon asked for wisdom to rule the nation of Israel (2 Chron.11, 12). It pleased God, so He added riches to Solomon's wisdom. In your caring situation, what do you ask God to do for you? The choices a caregiver makes may have far reaching implications on her or his caring. In your prayers, ask God for wisdom to help you meet the needs of others. God does not delight in selfish or self-centered requests.

The question is not only, what are you doing for others, but when someone has a need, do you evaluate the need before you respond?

Lord, help me use Your wisdom at my disposal in evaluating and responding to the needs of others. Amen!

————◆————

"There are no shortcuts to any place worth going."

—Beverly Sills

"But you, be strong and do not let your hands be weak, for your work shall be rewarded" (2 Chronicles 15.7).

"Pleasant sights and good reports give happiness and health" (Proverbs 15.30; TLB).

The Joy of Caring

Men and women who are involved in caring for others usually speak of the joy, satisfaction and fulfillment caring brings into their lives. They will admit that there is never a dull moment in caring. The shear drama, excitement and suspense constantly keep caregivers on their toes.

My former classmate in nursing school loved caring for premature babies. There was a particular baby that was barley over three pounds at birth. She made it her mission that this child would survive in a rural West African hospital. During rounds in the morning, medical and nursing staff gathered around Nurse Rachael to hear her progress reports on the baby. She was always dramatic and suspenseful about the baby's progress. She would say, "I will give you further details in the morning as the baby progresses."

The day came when the baby was finally discharged and handed over to her proud parents. Through caring, she proved the doctors and medical experts wrong that the premature baby would never survive. The power of caring may prove pundits wrong.

The moment you start caring, you are on your way to power, joy, success and fulfillment. Caring infuses you with joy. It interjects an internal dimension into an otherwise routine and mundane day of caring. This is one reason no one could not pay me enough money not to care for others.

Thank You, Lord for Your amazing power in caring. You made me a cheerful caregiver at salvation. Amen!

———— ♦ ————

"Joy comes from seeing the complete fulfillment of the specific purpose for which I was created and born again, not from successfully doing something of my own choosing."

—Oswald Chambers

"Blessed are the merciful for they shall obtain mercy" (Matthew 5.7).

"He who shows mercy, with cheerfulness" (Romans 12.8b).

"And when James, Cephas, and John, who seemed to be pillars, perceived the grace that had been given to me, they gave me and Barnabas the right hand of fellowship, that we should go to the Gentiles and they to the circumcised. They desired only that we should remember the poor, the very thing which I also was eager to do" (Galatians 2.9-10).

"Let all bitterness, wrath, anger, clamor, and evil speaking be put away from you with all malice. And be kind to one another, tenderhearted, forgiving one another, even as God in Christ forgave you" (Ephesians 4.32).

Caring Changes One's Perspective on Life

To watch caregivers respond to the needs of others is to see the gift of mercy (Rom 12.8b), at its most sublime, all speed, vision and holistic grace. It is a sight that even the most matured Christian may find hard to put into words. If you watched Christian caregivers respond to the victims of the World Trade Centers, Hurricane Andrews, and the Asian Tsunami, you would know what I am talking about. The only description I come up with is a lot of appreciation for Christians being led by the Holy Spirit to bring comfort and healing to the wounded and afflicted through caring. They relate, even to people with disability with compassion, love and hope for the future. They value and promote life itself.

The famous American writer, Og Mandino said this, "Beginning today, treat everyone you meet as if they were going to be dead by midnight. Extend to them all care, kindness, and understanding you can muster, and do it with no thought of any reward. Your life will never be the same again."

Caring is also considered sacred. It can be done to the glory of God. Caregivers who see caring as a gift through which they can serve God, gain a whole new perspective. They care for others as unto the Lord (Col 3.17).

Caring for others can dramatically change your perspective on life. Life takes on new meanings when God through His Spirit helps you to touch the life of someone who is hurting or afflicted.

Lord, use me to bring hope and a promising future to those who are afflicted and hurting. With You, there is hope. Amen!

————————◆ ◆————————

"I expect to pass through life but once. If, therefore, there be any kindness I can show, or any good thing I can do to any fellow being, let me do it now, and not defer or neglect it, as I shall not pass this way again."

—William Penn

"And let us not grow weary while doing good, for in due season, we shall reap if we do not lose heart. Therefore, as we have opportunity, let us do good to all, especially to those who are of the household of faith" (Galatians 6.9-10).

When You Think You have Failed to Care, or Burned Out in Caring

In the caregiving business it is not unusual to feel that you have failed or burned out. Since caregivers are called to bear the pains and suffering of others, it is no wonder that you and I feel burned out.

I am a great believer that hurting people everywhere need the healing touch of God's servants. The Bible encourages Christians "not to grow weary while doing good." When you do your best to care for thankless folks, it may also crush your spirit emotionally. It may seem as though the caregiver is required to beg for "thank you" for caring.

When we are emotionally drained, we may not be able to articulate our sense of failure or burnout. But the Bible also encourages us that "in due season, we will reap the reward for our work if we do not lose heart. No work of God is ever wasted. God values our good works for His people.

When God sent Moses back to Egypt to bring the Israelites out, he was accompanied by a backup. Moses' brother Aaron went along as a backup (Exod 4.1-17). Many teammates are never in the starting line-up on a team. At different times, God sends us mentors, guides, helpers and burden-bearers. They can assist us in caring. Before you burn out, look around for those helpers whom God may have sent your way.

Lord, help me be emotionally strong as a caregiver. Amen!

———— ◆ ————

"The probability that we may fail in the struggle ought not to deter us from the support of a cause we believe to be just."

—*Abraham Lincoln*

"And so it was on the next day that Moses sat to judge the people; and the people stood before Moses from morning until evening. So when Moses's father-in-law saw all that he did for the people, he said, "What is this thing that you are doing for the people? Why do you alone sit and all the people stand before you from morning until evening?" So Moses' father-in-law said to him, "The thing that you do is not good. Both you and these people who are with you will surely wear yourselves out. For this thing is too much for you; you are not able to perform it by yourself" (Exodus 18.13-14, 17–18).

"And Moses said, "The people whom I am among are six hundred thousand men on foot;" yet you have said, I will give them meat that they may eat for a whole month. "Shall flocks and herds be slaughtered for them to provide enough for them? Or shall all the fish of the sea be gathered together for them to provide enough for them"? And the Lord said to Moses, "Has the Lord's arm been shortened? Now you shall see whether what I say will happen to you or not" (Numbers 11.21-23).

"Now the Passover, a feast of the Jews was near. Then Jesus lifted His eyes, and seeing a great multitude coming toward Him, He said to Phillip, "Where shall we buy bread that these may eat?" But this He said to test him, for He Himself knew what He would do. Phillip answered Him, "Two hundred denarii worth of bread is not sufficient for them, that every one of them may have a little to eat" (John 6.4-7).

The Feeling of Inadequacy in Caring

Personal emotion may prevent a caregiver from asking for help when he or she may be overwhelmed with what to do. "I want to do it alone so I can claim all credits." "I do not want any distractions, or interferences from others." "It is good to feel inadequate by yourself." "It is embarrassing when others are around."

At times we all feel like Moses or Phillip when we are confronted with a caring situation that seems beyond our capability. "Lord, it will cost a fortune to meet the needs of these people." That is exactly what Moses and Phillip said.

God's resources at our disposal are limitless. They include people as well as materials. If and when we ask God, He makes them available to us. Before the feeling of inadequacy begins to creep in, ask God to make His resources available to you.

God is aware of every caregiver's limitation and encourages him or her to lighten the load by delegating responsibility to others who can help to make caring productive and effective. The primary caregiver always carries greater responsibility, but he or she can alleviate the stress of going at it alone by sharing the load. He or she should consider his or her responsibilities and how the caring responsibilities can be delegated to others in order to get the job well done.

The feeling of inadequacy may be a trick of the devil in order to shake the caregiver's confidence in God. Before God presents a caregiver with a need, He already knows exactly how He will meet the need through the caregiver. When a caregiver has confident in God, He will never allow the caregiver to fail. God does not fail! He cares through a caregiver to bring glory to His own name.

Lord, help me maintain my confidence in You. If I allow You to work through me, I will never feel inadequate to care. Amen!

———•◆•———

"Whoever has a heart full of love always has something to give."

—Pope John XXIII

"And let us not grow weary while doing good, for in due season, we shall reap if we do not lose heart. Therefore, as we have opportunity, let us do good to all, especially to those who are of the household of faith" (Galatians 6.9-10).

"But what I do, I will also continue to do that I may cut off the opportunity from those who desire an opportunity to be regarded just as we are in things of which they boast" (2 Corinthians 11.12).

"Do all things without complaining and disputing that you may become blameless and harmless, children of God without fault in the midst of a crooked and perverse generation, among whom you shine as lights in the world" (Philippians 2.14-15).

When You Feel Compassion-Fatigued

In the early 1980's, the phrase, "Compassion-Fatigued" became household words in Liberia. Many Liberians, including me, were repeatedly told that Americans were simply tired of helping Africans. Americans just did not have the resources anymore to care for anybody, except for themselves.

The word "compassion" is defined as "The feeling for another's sorrow or hardship that leads to help" (*The World Book Dictionary*). And the word, "fatigue" is defined as, "Weariness caused by hard work or effort. A task or exertion producing weariness" (*The World Book Dictionary*).

After nearly thirty-one years in the United States of America, combining the two definitions above; compassion and fatigued, seems like begging the question. The compassion of American Christians has not fatigued. Compassion is one of good works produced by the indwelling Holy Spirit (Gal 5.22; 1 Pet 3.8). Therefore, compassion can never be fatigued because God is never tired of doing good.

A Christian caregiver sees every person as a child of God, therefore, compassion is never defined with fatigue, rather in its proper context as an empathy for those who need help. That's God approved definition. When the Apostle Paul was shipwrecked on the Island of Malta, he continued to care. He never focused on himself. His compassion on the official of the island changed the man's life. As a caregiver, never underestimate what God can do through your compassion shown to others.

Caring for others is like dropping a large stone into a standing lake. Its ripples effect can touch lives in every corner of the globe. The ripples effect of Christian compassion is felt in poor and developing countries of the world daily.

Lord, in caring, help me define my compassion without fatigue. Amen!

"But those who trust in the Lord for help will find their strength renewed. They will rise up on wings like eagles; they will run and not get weary; they will walk and not grow weak" (Isaiah 40.31; GNT).

———◆———

"The word impossible is not in my dictionary."

—*Napoleon Bonaparte*

"But I rejoiced in the Lord greatly that now at last your care for me has flourished again; though you surely did care, but you lacked opportunity. Nevertheless you have done well that you shared in my distress. Now you Philippians know also that in the beginning of the gospel, when I departed from Macedonia, no church shared with me concerning giving and receiving but you only. For even in Thessalonica you sent aid once and again for my necessities" (Philippians 4.10, 14-16).

"Therefore, as the elect of God, holy and beloved, put on tender mercies, kindness, humility, meekness, longsuffering" (Colossians 3.12).

God Makes You a Fantastic Caregiver

Talk is real cheap. Speaking of caring is as easy as 1-2-3, but it is entirely another matter to live and breathe caring. The book of Leviticus spells out exact ways by which God people could express their commitments to Him. The sacrifices were costly, but the Israelites had to do them to get right with God. The sacrifices were words in actions. Believers today live their faith by their actions. The Bible declares, "Let us not love in word or in tongue, but in deeds and truth" (1 John 3.18).

Miss Lois Olsen went to Liberia as a short term missionary in 1980. She served at the nursing school in teaching and revising the curriculum of the nursing program.

One day a graduate of the nursing school was accepted for a two-month program in Maternal-Infant Health and Family Planning at the Emory University School of Nursing in Atlanta, Georgia. The graduate had no idea where to raise the first couples of dimes for the round-trip plane ticket.

Miss Olsen heard about the need. She called the graduate into her office and said to him, "I will pay for your round-trip ticket, but you must promise to return to work at this hospital." The graduate said, "Definitely, I will return. It is a deal"!

This was my first trip to Atlanta, Georgia September 1980. When I arrived, I immediately fell in love with the city. And when I left December 1980, I promised to return to Atlanta to study. I returned September 1985, and have never left.

All this happened because one fantastic caring missionary woman saw an opportunity to care and responded. As I endeavor to reach out to others today, I believe God makes me a fantastic caregiver also. And I hope, He has done the same thing for you.

Lord, true success in caring is determined by what You make me. Your word to me this day is to care. Just show me the need. Amen!

———◆———

"When you were born, you cried and the world rejoiced. Live your life in such a manner that when you die the world cries and you rejoice."

—Anonymous

Caring with a Pure Heart

"Now all who believed were together, and had all things in common, and sold their possessions and goods, and divided them among all, as anyone had need" (Acts 2.44-45).

"But all their works they do to be seen by men. They make their phylacteries broad and enlarge the borders of their garments" (Matthew 23.5).

"And not only that, but we also glory in tribulations, knowing that tribulation produces perseverance; and perseverance, character; and character, hope" (Romans 5.3-4).

"Don't be selfish; don't live to make a good impression on others. Be humble, thinking of others as better than yourself" (Philippians 2.3; TLB).

"Let no one despise your youth, but be an example to the believers in word, in conduct, in love, in spirit, in faith, in purity" (1 Timothy 4.12).

Character and Behavior Matter in Caring

A West African lady tells a story of helping her fellow men
and women who fled into a neighboring countries as refugees.
She fed and clothed their kids in the refugee camp. When she
was granted permission to resettle in the United States, she
brought some of the kids.

Somehow she is disappointed that the parents of these kids
do not appreciate how much she cares about their kids. In
fact, some of the older children do not relate to her as before.
They are now independent, and do not need her assistance.

Caring and compassionate people get easily hurt because they
empathize so much with the suffering of others. What they
do for others, and how they do them, matter very much.
Character and behavior matter in caring as much as caring
itself. In other words, caregivers set examples for others to
follow in caring.

In Caring we reveal what we are really made of. The actions

and attitudes of caregivers speak volume about their genuineness. Caregivers' attitudes are also reflected within their dedication to caring. There is nothing worse than caregivers with bad attitudes who do not get along with others or each other. Caregivers who are always nagging about workloads, exhaustion, and everything else make everyone uneasy and irritable in the caring business (Prov 19.13, 14). Caregivers with bad attitudes can renew their minds (Rom 12.1-2) and experience the transforming power of the Holy Spirit.

And manipulating the needs of others in order to gain notoriety may bring despair rather than hope. The Pharisees were known for such behavior. Therefore, Christ cautioned His disciples not to be like the Pharisees (Matt 23.15).

It does not matter how caregivers give, if they have character deficits, the caring ministry will not go far. There will be friction, even with those in need of care.

Lord, I want the right character and behavior in my caring. I want to be genuine in all that I do in caring for others. Amen!

———— • ————

"Character is doing what's right when nobody's looking."

–J.C. Watts

"Therefore we make it our aim, whether present or absent to be well pleasing to Him. For we must all appear before the judgment seat of Christ, that each one may receive the things done in the body, according to what he has done, whether good or bad" (2 Corinthians 5.9-10).

"And I saw the dead, small and great, standing before God, and books were opened. And another book was opened, which is the Book of Life. And the dead were judged according to their works, by the things which were written in the books. The sea gave up the dead who were in it, and the Death and Hades delivered up the dead who were in them. And they were judged, each one according to his works" (Revelation 20.12-13).

"Now Jabez was more honorable than his brothers, and his mother called his name Jabez, saying, "Because I bore him in pain." And Jabez called on the God of Israel saying, "Oh, that you would bless me indeed and enlarge my territory, that your hand would be with me, and that I may not cause pain." So God granted him what he requested" (1 Chronicles 4.9-10).

"That good thing which was committed to you, keep by the Holy Spirit who dwells in us" (2 Timothy 1.14).

"And who is he who will harm you if you become followers of what is good? But even if you should suffer for righteousness' sake, you are blessed. *And do not be afraid of their threats, nor be troubled.* But sanctify the Lord God in your hearts, and always be ready to give a defense to everyone who asks you a reason for the hope that is in you, with meekness and fear; having a good conscience that when they defame you as evildoers, those who revile your good conduct in Christ may be ashamed. For it is better, if it is the will of God to suffer for doing good than for doing evil" (1 Peter 3.13-17).

Caring without Causing Pain

A hurting individual is often in desperate situations. He or she may be in severe pain, or may have been traumatized by other individuals. His or her sense of independence may have been assaulted by traumatic events. And the reason he or she is in pain may never make any sense to a caregiver.

Knowing the caring world is essential to caregiving. An outsider may not be effective as a caregiver. Therefore, it is important for the care-er to know the individuals for whom he or she cares, where and why he or she cares, and what he or she does. The latter deals with the specifics of caring. It is not easy being a perpetual volunteer. A caregiver is a lifetime volunteer whose contracts never runs out. In this impatient and fast-paced world, caring is a never-ending undertaking.

Yet it is paramount for the caregiver to avoid causing further pain. Conforming to the image of Jesus Christ is looking for an opportunity to relieve pain and suffering. He did not hesitate to relieve a grief-stricken mother's pain by raising her son back to life. In other words, Christ wants caregivers' identities to be aligned with His.

In this context, when caring for seniors and the elderly, remember that God's laws prohibit Christian caregivers abusing or disrespecting them. They are to be treated with honor and respect. For Christian caregivers with God's laws in their hearts, there is no excuse for physical, verbal or any other abuse of seniors and the elderly (Lev 19.32).

Following Christ's examples in doing good may not necessarily win praise from the world, but the caregivers' testimonies will remain intact. Christ will unconditionally approve of them, enlarge their caring territories and bless them indeed.

Create in me today a clean spirit, Lord. Smooth out my rough edges so that I may not cause further pain to hurting people. Help me keep my testimony and identity in You. Amen!

————————◆◆————————

"May all your troubles last as long as your New Year's resolutions."

—Joey Adams

Caring Is Not Performed-Based

As a young pastor, this was my idea of a church. You bring a group of Christians to together for worship on Sundays. At each worship service, a generous and robust offerings are collected. At the end of each service, the pastor and leaders evaluate the needs of the church family. And then, portions of the offerings are given to various family members according to their needs. What a radical idea for a church!

This was my first experience as a pastor, but I sensed immediately that something was wrong. This would be performance, and not ministry. My rational was that others would see and hear about our deeds and, then flock to our church. We would not be genuinely meeting the needs of God's people, but making public spectacles for the world to see. In other words, we would be performing in the name of caring.

Caring flows spontaneously from the heart of the caregiver. God knows the heart of the caregiver. Whether God is physically watching or not, the caregiver's desire is to please Him. There is nothing as rewarding as performance-free caring. When a caregiver allows Christ to live and work through him or her, caring becomes caring rather than performance.

Lord, one of these days, I will stand before You to give accounts of caring for others. I want to hear You say, "Well done, you good and faithful caring servant. Amen!

———— ◆ ————

"None preaches better than the ant, and she says nothing."

—Benjamin Franklin

"Now all things are of God who has reconciled us to Himself through Jesus Christ, and has given us the ministry of reconciliation, that is that God was in Christ reconciling the world to Himself, not imputing their trespasses to them, and has committed to us the word of reconciliation. Now then, we are ambassadors for Christ, as though God were pleading through us: we implore you on Christ's behalf, be reconciled to God" (2 Corinthians 5.18-20).

Reconciling Through Caring

Caring is a deliberate choice a Christian makes at salvation. Therefore, caring engages his or her heart and spirit. If he or she fails to see his or her obligation as an initiator of reconciliation, care will begin to wane. Any relationship a caregiver reconciles through caring today could his or hers tomorrow.

The power of caring lies in reconciliation, even the bitterest of enemies. Several years ago, I conducted reconciliation revival services. The services lasted for three days with coronation on Sunday. The Spirit of God moved in a mighty way in the congregation.

Because of one pastor's caring attitude, broken relationships were restored, and bitter enemies became allies and friends again. As former enemies cried and embraced, I could only thank God for giving us the ministry of reconciliation. The entire process was God's work from the beginning to the end.

Christ's death on the cross at Calvary made it possible for us to be reconciled to God. Those who have accepted His gift of reconciliation through Christ's death are enjoying being reconciled first to God, and then to each other.

Dear, Lord, thanks for Your reconciliation through Christ's death on the cross. I rejoice as I attempt to reconcile others through caring. Amen!

———————•◆•———————

"If I can stop one heart from breaking, I shall not live in vain; If I can ease one life the aching, or cool one pain, or help one fainting robin unto his nest again I shall not live in vain."

—Emily Dickinson

"Search me, O God, and know my heart" (Psalm 139.23).

"The heart is deceitful above all things, and desperately wicked; who can know it" (Jeremiah 17.9)?

"Let not become conceited, provoking one another, envying one another" (Galatians 5.26).

"Let nothing be done through selfish ambition or conceit, but in lowliness of mind let each esteem others better than himself. Let each of you look out not only for his own interests, but also for the interests of others" (Philippians 2.3-4).

The Hidden Enemy of Conceit

Amy and Jane are best friends. Amy has no money to buy groceries. She has been praying that God would provide, at least a bag of groceries. One day, Jane shows up at Amy's house with a bag of groceries. Amy receives the bag of groceries and begins to thank and praise God. As Amy runs around in the house praising God, Jane follows, repeatedly reminding her that God has nothing to do with the groceries whatsoever. She [Jane] provides the groceries, therefore deserves to be thanked. This was a skit performed by two young ladies at our church years ago.

God may use crisis to bring people to Himself. God may use the power of caring through a caregiver to remedy the situation. But when a caregiver relies exclusively on his pride and ability, caring may become fanciful. This may take genuineness out of caring.

The greatest enemy of any caregiver is conceit. It is difficult to deal with because it is hidden within. Conceit may give a caregiver a false sense of enablement apart from the indwelling power of the Holy Spirit.

Some of the happiest and most joyful people in the world are those who seek and find how to care for others. They are not conceited in all that they do.

In my caring help me rely on Your strength, Oh Lord. Take away from me the hidden spirit of conceit. Amen!

———— ◆ ————

"Conceit is the most incurable disease that is known to the human soul."

—Henry Ward Beecher

"To the weak I became as weak, that I might win the weak. I have become all things to all men that I might by all means save some" (1 Corinthians 9.22).

"Then Eliphaz the Temanite answered and said: Remember now, who ever perished being innocent? Or where were the upright ever cut off? Even as I have seen, those who plow and sow trouble reap the same. By the blast of God they perish, and by the breath of His anger they are consumed" (Job 4.1, 7-9).

"Do not be deceived, God is not mocked; for whatever a man sows that he will also reap. For he who sows to his flesh will of the flesh reap corruption, but he who sows to the Spirit will of the Spirit reap everlasting life" (Galatians 6.7-8).

Caring May Be Rendered Ineffective
by Playing on People's Emotions

I grew up in a legalistic church. Nothing bad would happen to Christians unless they have sinned. If a member was sick, the elders would demand confession as a prerequisite for caring. "If you do not tell us that you committed an adultery, or you have sinned against our Holy God, the church will not help you."

The power and nobility of caring ride on compassion, and not manipulation. There is no experimentation in caring. I am a firm believer that people in need want to know how much you care about them before they care about how much you know (I Pet 3.8).

Caring is meeting physical need as well as leading others to the Lord. Caring also involves teaching, discipling, encouraging other Christians, courtesy and respect, godly living as examples to others, building each other up, and lovingly and gently restoring each other. In reality, one caring Christian can lighten the burdens of an entire congregation.

Caring is much like bearing fruit. Have you taken a brief moment to evaluate your level of caring? Are you caring a lot? Somehow caring? Doing a little caring? No caring at all? Most often, Christians are known by how well they care for others rather than playing on their emotions.

Heavenly Father, help me be empathetic to the suffering of others. I want to be humble and gentle in my caring. Amen!

———— ♦ ————

"If you can't help them, don't hurt them. If you can't care for them, don't crush them emotionally."

Dr. Peter Z.M. Nehsahn

"Now Michal, Saul's daughter loved David. And they told Saul, and the thing pleased him. So Saul said, "I will give her to him that she may be a snare to him, and that the hand of the Philistines may be against him." Therefore Saul said to David a second time, "You shall be my son-in-law." And Saul commanded his servants, "Communicate with David secretly and say, look the king has delight in you, and all his servants love you. Now therefore, become the king's son-in-law" (I Samuel 18.20-22).

"If your enemy is hungry, give him bread to eat; and if he is thirsty, give him water to drink; for so you will heap coals of fire on his head and the Lord will reward you" (Proverbs 25.21-22).

"Love your enemies, do good, and lend, hoping for nothing in return; and your reward will be great, and you will be sons of the Most High" (Luke 6.35).

"Bless those who persecute you; bless and do not curse" (Romans 12.14).

Caring with no String Attached

The following incidence is unique in this context. My wife and I knew a Christian family in Atlanta in the late 1980's. I had just completed my driving test, and was searching for a car. The family decided to give us a car as a gift. The car has a lot of problems. It got very expensive to maintain it. Therefore, my wife and I decided to sell it and use the money as down payment on another car.

I called the family and got their approval for the sale. They told me, "Go ahead and sell the car. It is yours now!" On the day of the sale, the head of the family sat as a witness.

I sold the car for $600.00. He took the money, took out $400.00, and handed me $200.00. My wife and I were awe-struck. We sat with our mouths opened for at least two minutes. We finally looked at each other and said to the man, "Thank you, sir!"

What would you have done? We were not upset or mad. We

thought it would had been better for the family to ask us to return the car.

King Saul did not care about David's singleness. He wanted David dead, therefore, he [Saul] was willing to use Michal, his daughter, as a snare of entrapment. Ask God to help you care with no string attached.

Lord, take this heavy load of caring with string attached from me. I am tired because it affects my ability to care. Amen!

———◆———

"Sincerity is impossible, unless it pervade the whole being, and the pretence of it saps the very foundation of character."

—-James Russell Lowell

Learning from the Master Through Listening and Spending Time with Him in Caring

"Be anxious for nothing, but in everything by prayer and supplication, with thanksgiving, let your requests be made known to God; and the peace of God which surpasses all understanding will guard your hearts and minds through Christ Jesus" (Philippians 4.6-7).

"Cast your burden on the Lord, and He shall sustain you; He shall never permit the righteous to be moved" (Psalm 55.22).

"Why are you downcast, O my soul? Why so disturbed within me? Put your hope in God, for I will yet praise Him, my Savior and my God" (Psalm 42.5; NIV).

"What a glorious Lord! He who daily bears our burdens also gives us our salvation" (Psalm 68.19; TLB).

Turning the Burdens Over to Him

My grandaunt's husband was an older man who suffered Polio as a young man. He could barely move his legs. He literally dragged himself when he walked. He used a single pair of crutch to walk.

He was a very energetic and strong man. As long as he was balanced on that one pair of crutch under his left arm, he performed any task imaginable. When he put the crutch away, he could not even stand. When Tokpa leaned on the crutch, he was invincible. The crutch was his weight and burden bearer.

When we lean on God, and turn the burdens of caring to Him, He strengthens us to care. Today if you cast your burdens of caring on Him, He will sustain you. He promises to bear our burdens daily.

In our desire to truly care, we may take on the life of the person in need. Being empathetic is not taking on the entire responsibility of the person who needs care. It means objectively putting yourself in his place and allowing God to work through you in meeting the need.

The best place to begin the objective process is with the Lord. Before caring becomes a burden, place the situation in the Hands of the Man from Galilee. He has answers to all of life's complex caring problems.

Lord, remind me daily to turn my burdens of caring over to You. You did not call me to bear burdens, but to care. Amen!

———— ◆ ————

"*Give me a task too big, too hard for human hands, then I shall come at length to lean on Thee, and leaning, find my strength.*"

—Witt Fowler

"For my thoughts at not your thoughts, nor are your ways my ways, says the Lord. For as the heavens are higher than the earth, so are my ways higher than your ways, and my thoughts than your thoughts" (Isaiah 55.8-9).

"Call to me, and I will answer you and show you great and mighty things which you do not know" (Jeremiah 33.3).

"Continue earnestly in prayer, being vigilant in it with thanksgiving; meanwhile praying also for us that God would open to us a door for the word, to speak the mystery of Christ, for which I am also in chains, that I may make it manifest as I ought to speak" (Colossians 4.2-4).

Accepting the Answer to Your Prayers to Care

When it comes to caring, God will answer a caregiver's prayers in one of four ways: 1) "Yes, caregiver, you may go ahead and respond to this particular need at this time," 2) "No, caregiver, this caring situation is beyond your control. You may not appropriately or adequately meet this need," 3) "Wait, caregiver, I do have a better caring situation for you that will bring glory to My Name," 4) "I want you to work in My strength so that you may not experience burnout. My grace is there when you need it. It is sufficient for all caring situations."

God always places us in caring situations where we will make the most impact. If we are praying and listening to His voice, He will not deliberately subject us to failure.

Therefore, before we respond to a caring need, calling first on God will be the right thing to do. His ways are perfect than ours. In His infinite wisdom, He may desire an outcome of a caring situation we may not know.

Lord, help me discern Your voice in waiting and responding in caring for others. I know if I listen as I pray, You will place me in a caring situation where I can make the most impact for You. Amen!

———————◆———————

"Lord, help live from day to day in such a self-forgetful way, that even when I kneel to pray, my prayer shall be for-others."

—Charles D. Meigs

"He saw that there was no man, and wondered that there was no intercessor; therefore, His own arm brought salvation for Him; and His own righteousness, it sustained Him" (Isaiah 59.16).

"Meanwhile praying also for us that God would open to us a door for the word, to speak the mystery of Christ, for which I am also in chains, that I may make it manifest as I ought to speak" (Colossians 4.2-4).

"Therefore I exhort first of all that supplications, prayers, intercessions and giving of thanks be made for all men" (I Timothy 2.1).

"Confess your trespasses to one another and pray for one another that you may be healed. The effective fervent prayer of a righteous man avails much" (James 5.16).

Fulfilling the Role as an Intercessor
for Those Who Desire to Care

Throughout the world, there are thousands of Christians who are praying daily for peace, the afflicted, healing, love, compassion, missionaries and salvation for all sinners.

When you and I are not able to respond to a specific need, God will raise up doctors, nurses, nurse assistants and other healthcare workers to do so. Our part is to be intercessors for those whom God has raised up to care. These caregivers may be in your church, community, neighborhood, or school.

The role of an intercessor is integral to any caring ministry. The intercessor stands in the gap; literally interceding in prayer on behalf of those who desire to care. We ask the Lord to help them respond in love and compassion. Frankly, a compassionate person is an intercessor.

We ask the Lord to help them care without preference for

race, nationalities, ethnicity, socio-economic, religious or denominational backgrounds. We ask the Lord to help them respond to all needs, and not selectively. These include spiritual as well as physical needs. We ask the Lord to help them plan and respond to immediate and long term needs accordingly. We ask the Lord to help the caregivers have the mind of Christ, and the same mind in caring.

Lord, grant caregivers the mind of Christ so that they may care with one accord to glorify Your name. Amen!

"So I sought for a man among them whom would make a wall, and stand in the gap before Me on behalf of the land that I should not destroy it; but found no one" (Ezekiel 22.30).

"And when He had sent the multitude away, He went up on the mountain by Himself to pray. Now when evening came, He was alone there" (Matthew 14.23).

"And when He had sent them away, He departed to the mountain to pray" (Mark 6.46).

"However, the report went around concerning Him all the more; and great multitudes came together to hear, and to be healed by Him of their infirmities. So he Himself often withdrew into the wilderness and prayed" (Luke 5.15-16).

"Now it came to pass in those days that He went out to the mountain to pray, and continued all night in prayer to God" (Luke 6.12).

Starting the Caring Day with God

One of the best times I enjoyed in nursing school was the early morning Chapel Services. When students arrived, the director stressed the importance of the Chapel Services. "In order to be an effective caregiver, begin your day with God. Every caregiver's greatest need is personal compassion. And compassion comes only from God."

I enjoyed chapel so much that I was appointed as one of the coordinators. I preached and led chapel services on many occasions. Beginning my caring day with God, made a great difference in how I responded to those who were ill and in pains. Frankly, those chapel services molded by thinking into becoming a Christian health worker. Have I attained my ultimate goal yet? No, but I am still working on it.

During His earthly ministry, our Lord Jesus Christ took time to pray to the Father. Every major decision was preceded by prayer to the Father. The appointment of the twelve disciples was preceded by an all-night prayer until in the morning (Luke 6.12-16).

Caring is a major undertaking. You will enjoy it by starting with the Father. As Martin Luther once said, "It is a good thing to let prayer be the first business of the morning and the last of the evening."

Father, remind me to begin my daily caring with You. I know a caring day begun with You will always be bright. Amen!

———◆———

"Begin and end the day with him who is Alpha and Omega, and if you really experience what it is to love God, you will redeem all the time you can for his more immediate service."

--Susanna Wesley—

"He said to them, "Come aside by yourselves to a deserted place and rest a while." For there were many coming and going, and they did not even have time to eat" (Mark 6.31).

"However, the report went around concerning Him all the more; and great multitudes came together to hear, and to be healed by Him of their infirmities. So he Himself often withdrew into the wilderness and prayed" (Luke 5.15-16).

It Pays to Have a Quiet Time with God

Today's society is as noisy as ever before. Many motorists drive with blaring music in their cars. When you come to traffic lights, or a stop sign, the motorist behind or in front you can almost make you fall out of your car. Vibrations can be terribly deafening.

Jesus and His disciples were always followed by great multitudes of people. Multitudes who needed constant care and attention. The Bible says the disciples did not even have time to eat (Mark 6.31). Yet the Master encouraged them to take time off and be by themselves. Why did He often call them aside? To rest, recharge and refresh themselves. A hectic caring schedule can take a physical, emotional and spiritual toll on caregivers. Our Lord knows that we need to rest when we are caring so that we would not burn out. He promises to refresh us so we can continue to care. Time spent refreshing and resting is not time wasted (Mark 6.31-32).

In the caring ministry, caregivers are better refreshed and sharp when they take time off. They spend quiet time with God so that they are well rested and ready to care.

A regular quiet daily devotional time set aside to talk and listen to God is greater than a shot of any stimulant. It carries the caregiver the entire day without refill or another shot.

In the noisiness of today's world, God wants us to "Be still and know that He is God" (Psalm 46.10). We can silently depend on Him for every caring opportunity.

Lord, grant me the earnest desire to spend time with You. I want to be called a true friend of Yours in my caring. Amen!

"Evening and morning and at noon I will pray, and cry aloud, and He shall hear my voice" (Psalm 55.17).

Resisting the Pressures and Temptations to Quit Caring

The pressures and temptations we experience in caring for others begin to dissipate when we are secluded, silent, and still before the Lord. It seems like we are all connected to pressure tanks and our lives are filled with anxieties, frustrations and the temptations to quit caring for others. As we focus on God, He unplugs our pressure tanks to drain. The draining reduces our anxiety, tension and frustration levels to such extend that we take comfort and confidence in the God. Continuous biblical medication will eventually empty the tanks and give us renewed spirits, minds and bodies.

We may be tired, weary, and emotionally distraught, but spending time alone with God brings renewed energy, power and strength for each caring task.

Beware that caring has its moments of highs and lows. Most often, the lows come just after what seemed like your best day. You may have done excellently in one caring situation, and soon you find yourself at the bottom of the mountain or in a valley. The lows are important deterrents to keep things in perspective that all glory belongs to God. When you celebrate your caring victory, remember your Creator (I Kgs 19.1-8).

"No temptation has overtaken you except such as is common to man; but God is faithful, who will not allow you to be tempted beyond what you are able, but with the temptation will also make the way of escape, hat you may be able to bear it" (! Corinthians 10.13).

Lord help me handle the pressures and temptations of this life. Please refresh me daily for the caring tasks ahead of me. Help me right now and renew my strength so I can be effective in caring for others. Amen!

Our God Is a True Dream Giver

"And Joseph's brothers came and bowed down before him with their faces to the earth. So Joseph recognized his brothers, but they did not recognize him. Then Joseph remembered the dreams which he had dreamed about them, and said to them, "You are spies! You have come to see the nakedness of the land!" (Genesis 42.6b, 8-9).

"Commit your work to the Lord, then it will succeed" (Proverbs 16.3; TLB).

"When a man is trying to please God, God makes even his worst enemies to be at peace with him" (Proverbs 16.7; TLB).

"Behold, I am the Lord, the God of all flesh. Is there anything too hard for Me" (Jeremiah 32.27)?

Allow God to Change Your Dream of Caring into Reality

When Thomas Masse entered a nursing school in rural Eastern Liberia in the late 1970's, he had one dream. He wanted a career in nursing so he could make a lot of money. He envisioned having his own drugstores all over the country, with other nurses working for him. He wanted to be his own boss. It was a great ambition!

One day his dream came crashing down because his desire to care for others was outweighed by the desire to make a lot of money. I can record the day he left. He wept bitterly because he did not attain his dream.

Caring is not exactly about making a lot of money. God blesses those who have taken up the noble task of caring for others. He will meet whatever need a caregiver may have.

Every calling in life may not necessarily be about money. It is primarily about passion and love, and secondarily about money. When riches become the reasons for caring, the caregiver may not greatly pursue the calling.

Is becoming a caregiver your dream? Have you committed this dream to the Lord? There is nothing too hard for our God.

Take a step of faith today. It will change your life forever. There is always something wonderful about a dream. God will either grant it, or mend it for His own glory.

Lord, my dream is to care. Grant me the passion as I prepare for the calling. Amen!

————— ◆ —————

"But that dream can die will be a thrust between my ribs forever of hot pain."

—Edna St. Vincent Millay

"Then He went out from there and came to His own country, and His disciples followed Him. And when the Sabbath had come, He began to teach in the synagogue. Many hearing Him were astonished, saying, "Where did this Man get these things? And what wisdom is this which is given to Him, that such mighty works are performed by His hands! Is this not the carpenter, the Son of Mary, and brother of James, Joses, Judas, and Simon?" So they were offended at Him. But Jesus said to them, "A prophet is not without honor except in His own country, among his relatives, and in his own house" (Mark 6.1-4).

"So He came to Nazareth , where He had been brought up. And as His custom was, He went into the synagogue on the Sabbath day, and stood up to read. And He was handed the book of the prophet Isaiah. And when He had opened the book, He found the place where it was written:

The Spirit of God is upon Me, Because He has anointed Me to preach the gospel to the poor; He has sent Me to heal the brokenhearted, to proclaim liberty to the captives and recovery of sight to the blind, to set at liberty those who are oppressed; to proclaim the acceptable year of the Lord.

"Then He closed the book and gave it back to the attendant and sat down. And the eyes of all who were in the synagogue were fixed on Him. And He began to say to them, "Today this Scripture is fulfilled in your hearing." So all bore witness to Him, and marveled at the gracious words which proceeded out of His mouth. And they said, "Is this not Joseph's son?" He said to them, "You will surely say this proverb to Me, Physician, heal yourself! Whatever we have heard done in Capernaum, do also here in Your country. Then He said to them, "Assuredly, I say to you, no prophet is accepted in his own country" (Luke 4.16-24).

The Challenge of Living up to the Dream of Caring

Before I came to the United States in 1985, I built a drugstore in my hometown. I have heard and seen terrible sufferings in this little town of barely 200 people. The infant death rate from childhood diseases such as Malaria, diarrhea, Whooping Cough, Measles and Pyrexia (fever with no known cause) in the town was staggering. I felt it was the right thing to do in order to help my people.

One day a friend arrived from Asia and saw me washing and bandaging kids' wounds, and handling out anti-malaria pills. He said to me, "I cannot believe you would stoop this low to wash and bandage wounds on these dirty kids. When and where did you learn to do all this stuff anyway" (he himself died of Hepatitis A three years ago)? I replied, "I enjoyed this very much because this is what God called me to do. At least, I am giving something back to our people."

Caring can be lonely. A caregiver can be lonely even when

surrounded by others. King David was lonely as a young man and as king of Israel (Ps 69.1-12). In your loneliness as a caregiver, make sure to be alone with God in prayer and meditation. When the courage to care fails, when other caregivers, friends, or family members say to you, "You are on your own," you can take comfort in knowing that God is always near. A Christian is never alone.

If you desire to care, friends and families may not like you very much. Caring may take you to some unsanitary, or unclean environment with very little reward or pay. People for whom you desire to care may even resent you.

You may face a few challenges from detractors in caring. When that happens, be encouraged because without challenges there is no excitement in caring.

Dear Father, please help me live my dream of caring. Grant me wisdom in dealing with my detractors. Amen!

"*Every calling is great when greatly pursued.*"

—Oliver Wendell Holmes

"My sheep hear My voice, and I know them, and they follow Me. And I give them eternal life, and they shall never perish; neither shall anyone snatch them out of My hand. My Father who has given them to Me is greater than all; and no one is able to snatch them out of My Father's hand. I and My Father are one" (John 10.27-30).

"You were bought at a price; do not become slaves of men. Brethren, let each one remain with God in that state in which he was called" (1 Corinthians 7.23-24).

"For all the promises of God in Him are Yes, and in Him Amen, to the glory of God through us. Now He who establishes us with you in Christ and has anointed us is God, who also has sealed us and given us the Spirit in our hearts as a guarantee" (2 Corinthians 1.20-22).

"Therefore submit to God. Resist the devil and he will flee from you. Draw near to God and He will draw near to you" (James 4.7-8a).

The Enemy May Attempt to Steal
Your Dream of Caring

While Andrew was cutting my hair, I said to him, "You and your coworkers enjoy what you do. You do have patience, too. Sometimes you spend at least thirty minutes trimming a guy's beard. A guy walks in this shop, and when he gets out, he looks better than when he came in." He replied, "I am not in this for the money. This is more than a hobby for me. I enjoy every minute of it."

As a kid I was repeatedly told, "Do not feel bad, even when you get an ugly haircut because it will grow back." When my grandfather or uncle cut my hair, he would push or slap my head around in order to make me sit still or straight.

But watch a true barber in action. He takes time and care to make sure his or her customers look good. A customers' haircuts are the barber's reputation. He keeps his customers coming back by caring for their hair.

Most great caring men and women in God's kingdom can point to a day in their lives when they made a formal decision to care for God's people. The enemy may attempt to steal that decisive dream away from them. But the keeping power of the Father is awesome. The enemy has no chance of taking them away from Him.

Dear Lord, thank You for constantly reminding me that I need to submit to You. When I obey, the devil will flee away from me and not attempt to steal my dream away. Amen!

————— ◆ —————

"The Bible knows nothing of a hierarchy of labor. No work is degrading. If it ought to be done, then is it good work"

—Ben Patterson

"These six things the Lord hates, Yes seven are an abomination to Him: A proud look, a lying tongue, hands that shed innocent blood, a heart that devices wicked plans, feet that are swift in running to evil, a false witness who speaks lies and one who sows discord among brethren" (Proverbs 6.16-19).

"Make no friendship with an angry man, and with a furious man do not go, lest you learn his ways and set a snare for your soul" (Proverbs 22.24-25).

"Do not be deceived: Evil company corrupts good habits" (1 Corinthians 15.33b).

Caring Dream Busters

Most illustrations in this book have to do with nursing because nurses are caring professionals. These men and women have given up nearly everything in life to care for the well-being of others.

Hansen Glenn left his parents' home in Northern Liberia and went to an eastern rural county to become a nurse. Mid way through his senior year, he began hanging out with the wrong crowd; men who were abusing narcotics (Demerol, Morphine and Minor Tranquilizers). Four weeks before graduation, he and the men were expelled from nurses training. It was a terrible blow to him, and to those who knew him as a friend. It was a great loss to the school also because Hansen was one of the brightest students in the school. What are caring dream busters?

- *Corrupt friends* - these men and women will eventually corrupt your mind and cause you to lose your dream. They may be referred to as **Dreamer Bully**.

- **Anger** - compassionate caring and anger do not mix. Wherever there is anger, there is bound to be resentment rather than love and caring.
- **Pride** - may poison a caregiver's heart and cause him or her not to respond adequately to the needs of others. Self-praise and boasting of one's accomplishments are usually the hallmarks of pride.
- **Lies** - wherever there are lies, care will be tainted with wrongful desires to extract restitutions from those in need. This may include stealing and demanding and receiving illegal gratuities.
- **Divisiveness** - Wherever there is division, there is infighting. The divisive person says, "Whether you are in need or pain, you are on your own."

Without caring dream busters, a caregiver may be at his or her very best. To Comfort someone who is hurting is a dream any individual may desire. It is a miraculous dream to meet the needs of hurting people. Never forget the Dream Giver who is your Father in heaven. He will strengthen and lead you throughout this dream

Lord, keep me away from all caring dream busters. When I stumble, give me strength to overcome them. Amen!

————•◆•————

"It was pride that changed angels into devils; it is humility that makes [us] as angels"

—*St. Augustine*

"You shall not take vengeance, nor bear any grudge against the children of your people, but you shall love your neighbor as yourself: I am the Lord" (Leviticus 19.18).

"Beloved, do not avenge yourselves, but rather give place to wrath; for it is written, "Vengeance is Mine, I will repay," says the Lord" (Romans 12.19).

"For we know Him who said, "Vengeance is Mine, I will repay," says the Lord. And again, "The Lord will judge His people." It is a fearful thing to fall into the hands of the living God" (Hebrews 10.30-31).

"Not returning evil for evil or reviling for reviling, but on the contrary blessing, knowing that you were called to this that you may inherit a blessing" (1 Peter 3.9).

Overcoming Revenge in Order to Truly Care

No matter what denomination a person belongs, one of the most difficult caring acts of the Christian faith is forgiveness. How do you forgive those who have repeatedly hurt you? How do you care for those who have been cruel to you?

Overcoming revenge in order to care is a challenge to the caregiver. This is where the caregiver's compassion is tested. Someone who has hurt you or your family is in desperate need, or in terrible pain. How do you respond, knowing that the innate tendency to retaliate resides within us all?

Corrie ten Boom's terrible experience in World War II, especially the cruel death of her sister led her to become a popular speaker on God's grace and forgiveness. She admitted, "After my long imprisonment, there was hatred in my heart, especially for the nurse who has been cruel to my sister Betsy."

The power to overcome revenge and care comes through divine power. We may choose to forgive, but God's Spirit empowers us to forgive and care. Friends, the desire for revenge can be so overpowering that without God's intervention, genuine forgiveness and caring may never take place. If anyone had a good reason for revenge, it was Joseph. His brothers' jealousy provoked them to horrible abuse, selling him as a common slave to foreigners (Gen 37.11-28). But Joseph forgave his brothers, and when a caring moment arose, he stepped up to the plate.

God through Christ Jesus has already forgiven the caregiver, therefore, God is asking him or her to forgive others. The chance to always forgive is ever before every caregiver. The process may be painful, but harboring resentment and bitterness is even hazardous to any caring ministry. When revenge becomes a caregiver's executioner, the caring dream may die a permanent death.

Lord, I know that revenge does not heal. Healing comes only as I learn to forgive and care. You already forgave me. Amen!

"Rejoice, O Gentiles, with His people; for He will avenge the blood of His servants and render vengeance to His adversaries; He will provide atonement for His land and His people" (Deuteronomy 32.43).

"Therefore, my beloved brethren, be steadfast, immovable, always abounding in the work of the Lord, knowing that your labor is not in vain in the Lord" (I Corinthians 15.58).

"Therefore we also, since we are surrounded by so great a cloud of witnesses, let us lay aside every weight, and the sin which so easily ensnares us, and let us run with endurance the race that is set before us" (Hebrews 12.1).

Caring for God's People Is a Dream Come True

A popular American speaker and grief educator tells a story of his Sunday school teacher who drove thirty miles to be at his grandfather's funeral although she did not know the deceased. She was there because a kid was a member of her Sunday school class.

As someone who has experienced so many deaths in the family, I was moved into tears by the story. How amazingly caring that a Sunday school teacher would drive thirty miles to comfort a kid at his grandfather's funeral! Every caregiver probably dreams of making such an impact on the life of a child.

No one can say, "I will care for twenty-one or thirty days, and then stop. Caring is an ongoing ministry. Until Jesus comes back, you, I, or somebody will always need care. The dream of caring is lived before thousands of witnesses each day.

There is a race before us to run until Christ comes back. Therefore, Christ desires caregivers to be steadfast, immovable, always abounding in caring. The caregivers' labor in the Lord is not in vain. There are crowns awaiting them at the finished line.

At the end of each caring day, the Master is waiting to cheer and congratulate every caregiver: "Well done, good and faithful servant. . ." (Matthew 25.21).

Lord, caring for Your people is a dream come true. Please help keep my dream in perspective, and not to lose it. Amen!

———•♦•———

"Dream big—dream very big. Work hard—very hard. And after you've done all you can, you stand, wait, and fully surrender"

--Oprah Winfrey—

Conclusion: Caring in Such a Time as This

"He who shuts his ears to the cries of the poor will be ignored in his own time of need" (Proverbs 21.13; TLB).

It has not been my intention to make you feel guilty in order to motivate you to care. This book is about every Christian's desire—the joy of caring. It is time to resurrect our compassion and put it into action. There are radical implications when compassion is in action. You will never be the same when you begin to care for others.

We may attempt to divorce caring and our faith, but Christ sees them as inseparable. Caring was central to His earthly ministry. Therefore, we are more like Christ when caring. When we focus on Him, we will become care-ers. When we care long enough, we will become like Him.

Caring is not an exclusive luxury of the rich and famous. It is a privilege granted to every Christian at salvation. I have personally come to know that there is joy in caring.

When Christians come together to talk about caring, they always express joy, excitement, and being wonderfully inspired by Christ to meet the needs of others.

In such a time as this, allow God to interrupt your daily routines with the needs of people. Ask God to constantly bring to your attention people with all kinds of needs. When that happens, take the time to care a lot. In such a time as this, it is a blessing to care a lot, listen carefully and complain less about the burdens of caring.

Allow me to paraphrase Acts 20.35 for you. "I have shown you by examples, living and working in your midst everyday so that you may support the weak. And remember what our Lord Jesus Christ says, "It is more blessed to care [give] than to receive" (Acts 20.35).

This book is not intended to be read for a specific number of days. It is a practical book for all caring seasons. Refer to it at all times in your caring. It will encourage you by reading it often as you meet the needs of God's people. And remember, *"There is Power in Caring."*

And if someone asks you as to what you did in your life that was so special? Smile and reply, I cared for God's people. I did not do it to gain notoriety, fame, honor, win a championship or a title. I cared because God through His Son Jesus Christ chose me and set me part to care. And I will keep on caring because Christian caring never quits. It keeps on caring until the Master Care-r returns!

Lord, this is my ultimate prayerful desire; to be a caring

person. You first loved and cared for me. Therefore, help me to do the same for others. Amen!

"Therefore, when Jesus saw her weeping, and the Jews who came with her weeping, He groaned in the spirit and was troubled. And He said, "Where have you laid him?" They said to Him, "Lord, come and see." Jesus wept. Then the Jews said, "See how He loved him!" And some of them said, "Could not this Man who opened the eyes of the blind, also have kept this man from dying" (John 11.33-37)?

CPSIA information can be obtained
at www.ICGtesting.com
Printed in the USA
FSHW012006201218
54615FS